German Shepherd

Puppy Training

Ashton Matthews

A Guide into the mind of a German Shepherd puppy and basic commands: Sit, Down, Stay, Come, Fetch, Potty Training, Bonding, Seeking and Speak

Table of Contents

About the Breed

Some say the German Shepherd "has a particular identity set apart by immediate and courageous, however not unfriendly, articulation, fearlessness, and a specific reserved quality that does not fit quick and unpredictable companionships. The canine must be receptive, discreetly holding fast and indicating certainty and eagerness to meet suggestions without itself making them."

That is an awesome depiction of a perfect German Shepherd. Lamentably, it's extremely hard to locate a perfect German Shepherd today. These days, this breed is everywhere in disposition. Lines that are reared for security work and the game of schutzhund have a tendency to be "hard-tempered" and efficient. Show lines extend from gentle and smooth, to hyperactive and touchy, to out and out imbecilic and dopey. What's more, numerous German Shepherds reared by lawn reproducers have hazardous demeanors and experience the ill effects of a large group of medical issues.

Vitality levels change from enthusiastic to laid-back, however all German Shepherds, to keep up their athletic shape, require lively strolling each day and hard and fast running in a protected, encased territory as frequently as would be prudent.

Mental exercise (propelled compliance classes, readiness classes, schutzhund, following, crowding) is much more critical for German Shepherds. This is a shrewd, thinking breed (at any rate the great ones are!) and his knowledge is regularly squandered in a home that basically needs an easygoing pet.

Schutzhund is a German word for protection dog. It alludes to a game that spotlights on creating and assessing those attributes in canines that make them more helpful and more joyful friends to their proprietors. Schutzhund work focuses on three sections which are Tracking, Obedience and Protection.

At long last, early and continuous socialization is an absolute necessity to build up a steady, sure disposition.

Most German Shepherds approve of other family pets, if presented when youthful. Be that as it may, a few people are feline chasers, and numerous people are prevailing or even forceful with interesting canines of a similar sex.

A standout amongst the most proficient and trainable breeds in all of dogdom, exceedingly anxious to learn and work, a perfect German Shepherd, when all around prepared by a sure proprietor, is a sublime partner.

This breed is outstanding for his drive to work, enthusiasm to satisfy you and his to a great degree high knowledge. It is this insight that can be revile on the off chance that you are not fit for preparing him to the degree that he needs with the goal that he can be a casual and all around carried on pet or working accomplice. Start preparing your puppy appropriate from the begin to set him up for progress and a grown-up canine buddy inside your family.

In the Beginning

1. Have a family meeting

A canine is a major responsibility, so before you dive in, ensure you're all together on needing this most up to date individual from the family. At that point choose who will be the essential caretaker– else you'll invest heaps of energy contending while your new canine gazes at his vacant nourishment bowl. To abstain from confounding the pup, work out the house manages early (will the canine be permitted on the bed? On the love seat? Where will the puppy rest? Are any rooms of the house for all time beyond reach?).

2. Stock up on the correct supplies.

Get a portion of the essentials early, so you both and your pooch can settle in without excessively numerous frantic dashes to the store. This is what you'll require: box, sustenance and water bowls also perhaps a few treats for preparing. Endeavor to get a similar sustenance your puppy's been simple since a sudden switch in eating regimen can irritate his stomach.

Other things you will need are: neckline and rope, bed toys, particularly bite toys, stain-and scent evacuating cleaners, potentially some infant entryways to close off areas of your home

3. Set up your home.

This requires somewhat more work in case you're getting a puppy, since they can be champion chewers and have a talent for getting into things they shouldn't. Be that as it may, regardless of what your pooch's age, you'll need to do some sorting out early.

Make a brief, gated-off living space for your canine or pup, where she can't harm your effects or eat something that will make her debilitated. She'll remain here at whatever point you're not with her to keep her from having house preparing mishaps.

Pick a room that is a focal point of action in your family, so your canine won't feel separated, and make sure it's unified with simple to-clean floors. The kitchen is frequently a decent decision; you can close it off with child entryways if necessary. Ensure you evacuate anything that you don't need bit on or ruined.

What's in your pooch's region will fluctuate a bit relying upon her age and how you're house preparing.

Puppy-verification to ensure anything that could hurt your dog– prescriptions, chemicals, certain plants– is distant.

The most punctual preparing your German Shepherd puppy should encounter is the means by which to cooperate with you, taking in his hindrances inside the home, house preparing and essential submission. This may seem like a considerable measure and you may feel overpowered, yet most by far of these are done during each time communications with your puppy. This incorporate nibble hindrance, learning tolerance and discretion and the more evident summons, for example, sit, down, stay and strolling pleasantly on a free chain.

Imprinting & Socializing

Mingling your German shepherd will be critical. Puppies that are not appropriately mingled can wind up plainly restless, dreadful, and forceful around different mutts as they become more established. This is particularly valid for the German shepherd, who is normally defensive and will normally need to shield your pack from outside impacts on the off chance that he is not shown that there is by and large no requirement for alert.

The most ideal way you could prepare a German Shepherd is by treating it in a sensible and positive way. Instructing your German Shepherd to be loyal towards you and your requests is not a simple undertaking. This kind of training needs a great deal of persistence and consistency. In the event that you lose your temper anytime amid the procedure, you and your pooch will both face a hard time.

Many focused on German Shepherd proprietors call preparing focuses to get hold of their pooch's temper. What they neglect to comprehend is that constraining their canine to learn and afterward getting forceful when it doesn't, is not the correct approach to do it.

There are two sections in submission preparing of a German Shepherd, and one of them is engraving and mingling. This sort of preparing incorporates a specific kind of traps and orders. Keep in mind, regardless of which style you embrace, you should utilize hand and verbal activities.

What is engraving? When you treat your German Shepherd pup irately amid its instructing, it is probably going to grow up to end up plainly a forceful canine. This is called engraving, as the puppy engraves the treatment it gets from the proprietor.

What is Socializing? Mingling a German Shepherd with individuals and different creatures in its encompassing is a noteworthy piece of its preparation. When you get a German Shepherd, you should make it agreeable around others with the goal that it doesn't cause inconveniences later on.

Obedience

German shepherds are to a great degree shrewd and dynamic puppies. Also, much the same as astute and dynamic human youngsters, they should be given both incitement and limits keeping in mind the end goal to be upbeat and balanced. Some German shepherd proprietors overlook (or maybe don't understand) that these expansive, dynamic mutts require compliance preparing.

Not on the grounds that they are awful mutts or hard to deal with, but since compliance preparing builds up you as the alpha in the pack. This ensures your shepherd knows the charges and flags that will keep him safe and will give him the structure that he wants.

In this piece of the preparation procedure, you should educate your German Shepherd to remain quiet and tune in to your summons expeditiously. German Shepherds are to a great degree vigorous and have a tendency to get energized effortlessly. That is the reason when you prepare them; they take after the orders in a hyperactive mode. To influence them to comprehend the significance of each summon and to initiate tolerance in them, you should mentor them in an unexpected way.

Potty Training

A couple of ventures of counteractive action can help avoid real issues later on. Start your puppy with box preparing to help in showing him potty propensities. This is effortlessly done by utilizing the carton just when you can't give 100% of your consideration on your puppy to forestall mishaps. Give him the chance to do his business in the right detect at regular intervals to a hour and up to 20 minutes in the wake of eating and drinking.

He ought to likewise be permitted to potty before anything else, last thing before sleep time during the evening, and previously, then after the fact preparing and play sessions. For each time your puppy goes potty in the right place, he ought to be adulated and remunerated. Giving a sustenance reward can help, yet it is not required to strengthen legitimate potty propensities.

Most puppies, if being prepared to dispose of outside, value a short play session outside after they potty. This not just fortifies the conduct of dispensing with in the right place, however it additionally shows them that going potty does not mean they should promptly backpedal inside. Proprietors of grown-up canines frequently report having a troublesome time getting their puppy to potty outside rapidly, as he would rather hold it and investigate outside. This is regularly due to being brought straightforwardly back inside in the wake of doing their business, so they attempt to put off doing what they're intended to do. By compensating with an outside play session, your puppy is discovering that on the off chance that he potties as soon as possible.

Fundamental Training Concept

Besides, your puppy ought to likewise be prepared in essential conduct, including acquiescence. This ought to likewise begin the day you bring him home, as he figures out how to communicate with you. Keep in mind that your puppy is only an infant. He was not conceived with the intrinsic capacity to comprehend your dialect and he assuredly does not recognize what is satisfactory and what is most certainly not.

This is dependent upon you to show him, for example, chomp restraint. The minute your puppy's teeth ever comes into contact with you, all diversions are finished. You should disregard him for a couple of minutes or totally end your connection with him all together for some time. This shows him that once his teeth touch you, what he needs, which is ordinarily play times or treats amid preparing, is finished. He is not being rebuffed, but rather he is not getting what he needs either.

This is known as a minimum strengthening situation, and he figures out how to settle on the decision to not touch his teeth to you to proceed with what he needs, for example, play.

Review

Your puppy ought to be knowledgeable in review and practice it frequently all through the primary couple of years of his life. Review is the point at which you call your canine's name and instruct him to come, and he drops everything without exception he is as of now doing to obey you. He will do this by decision in light of the fact that noting your review is much more strengthening than whatever else he could be doing, incorporating coming in soil, playing, burrowing or notwithstanding pursuing a squirrel. No go is instantly an ace at review, and it takes a great deal of consistency on your part to get it going.

Review is fundamental on the off chance that you ever mean to practice your puppy off chain or ever go to a canine stop. It is a security safety measure with the goal that you can get your puppy to move out of damages route before a mishap could happen, for example, pursuing a ball over a bustling street or staying away from a forceful canine at the recreation center. At the point when your puppy is dependable in review, he is sheltered to play off rope.

You can start educating your puppy review that week you bring him home! The prior the better, with the goal that you can establish a solid framework to expand upon as he develops into a youthful grown-up. Begin in a calm place that is recognizable to you and your pup with next to zero diversions. Inside your house is the best place to begin. You can start with your puppy on chain or not, that is totally up to you. On the off chance that you choose to utilize a chain, make sure to never put weight on it, don't reel your puppy in and don't jolt on it by any means!

You need him to figure out how to review, not react to rope weight presently. You can utilize a toy or treat that you know your puppy adores and essentially walk in reverse in an energized way. Call to him and urge him to tail you. When he makes up for lost time to you, compensate him! As he improves, you can build the criteria by including little diversions around him and move into another region.

When you settle on the choice to move outside and deal with review, he should be chained! This is for his security and to set him up to succeed. Begin off with a standard 6 foot rope, however as he gets on to coming to you as you walk in reverse you can put resources into a long line, more often than not in the vicinity of 15 and 30 feet long. The length is up to your inclination. Do an indistinguishable fundamental exercise from some time recently, and simply walk in reverse calling to your puppy. You can utilize a treat or toy to stand out enough to be noticed and compensate him with it when he comes to you.

When you are certain with his conduct, you can acquire an aide to chip away at the review amusement. In this preparation diversion you and your aide will remain around 10 feet separated from each other, as yet keeping your German Shepherd puppy on his long line. Both of you will have rewards prepared to provide for your puppy, and alternate calling him. When he gets to you, give him the reward, and reward him again to stay with you. He should remain with you until the point when you give the alright for your aide to call to him. Once more, they should compensate him for like clockwork he remains there.

You would prefer not to compensate him for coming and afterward taking off once more, however to come when called and remain with you!

As your puppy develops and you two acquire trust in his review capacities you can begin taking him off chain and chipping away at review without it. Begin to include more diversions. Utilize just basic ones in the first place, for example, a couple of toys laying on the ground, at that point make them harder.

Remember, however, to never go past your pooch's capacities. Construct and expand on what he can do, however don't test him by making it excessively troublesome, which could set you back in preparing. This goes for any orders you educate your puppy! On the off chance that anytime he appears to come up short and deteriorate, the time has come to make a couple of strides back and develop your way back.

Sit

Since you have the canine's consideration, hold the rope in your left hand and the nourishment treat in your privilege. Place your sustenance hand at the puppy's nose and let him lick the treat however not take it from you. Say "Sit" and gradually raise your nourishment hand from before the pooch's nose up finished his head with the goal that he is taking a gander at the roof.

As he twists his head upward, he should twist his knees to keep up his adjust. As he twists his knees, he will accept a sit position. By then, discharge the sustenance treat and acclaim sumptuously with remarks, for example, "Good boy! Great sit," and so forth. Make sure to dependably applaud energetically, in light of the fact that puppies savor verbal acclaim from their proprietors and feel so glad for themselves at whatever point they finish a conduct.

You won't utilize sustenance everlastingly in getting the canine to comply with your charges. Sustenance is just used to educate new practices, and once the canine comprehends what you need when you give a particular order, you will wean him off the nourishment treats yet at the same time keep up the verbal acclaim. All things considered, you will dependably have your voice with you, however there will be commonly when you have no nourishment compensates yet you anticipate that the pooch will comply.

Down

Educating the down exercise is simple when you see how the puppy sees the down position, and it is extremely troublesome when you don't. What's more, educating the down exercise utilizing the wrong strategy can in some cases influence the canine to grow such a dread of the down that he either flees when you say "Down" or he endeavors to chomp the individual who tries to compel him down.

Have the puppy sit close nearby your left leg, confronting in an indistinguishable course from you are. Hold the rope in your left hand and a sustenance treat in your privilege.

Presently put your left hand daintily on the highest point of the puppy's shoulders where they meet over the spinal line. Try not to push down on the canine's shoulders; just rest your left hand there so you can direct the puppy to rests near your left leg instead of to swing far from your side when he drops. Presently put the nourishment hand at the canine's nose, say "Down" delicately (very nearly a whisper) and gradually bring down the sustenance hand to the pooch's front feet. At the point when the sustenance hand achieves the floor, start advancing it along the floor before the puppy. Continue whispering to the pooch, saying things like, "Do you need this treat? You can do this, great puppy." Your consoling manner of speaking will help quiet the canine as he tries to take after the nourishment turn keeping in mind the end goal to get the treat.

At the point when the puppy's elbows touch the floor, discharge the nourishment and acclaim delicately. Endeavor to get the puppy to keep up that down position for a few seconds previously you let him sit up once more. The objective here is to get the canine to settle down and not feel undermined in the down position.

Stay

It is anything but difficult to educate the puppy to remain in either a sit or a down position. Once more, we utilize sustenance and acclaim amid the showing procedure as we help the puppy to see precisely what it is that we are anticipating that him should do.

To instruct the sit/stay, begin with the puppy sitting on your left side as earlier and hold the rope in your left hand. Have a sustenance treat in your correct hand and place your nourishment hand at the canine's nose. Say "Stay" and venture out on your correct foot to stand straightforwardly before the pooch, toe to toe, as he licks and snack the treat. Make sure to keep his head confronting upward to keep up the sit position. Tally to five and afterward swing around to remain beside the pooch again with him to your left side. When you return to the first position, discharge the sustenance and acclaim sumptuously.

To educate the down/stay, do the down as already portrayed. When the puppy rests, say "Stay" and venture out on your correct foot similarly as you did in the sit/remain. Tally to five and after that arrival to remain next to the canine with him on your left side. Discharge the regard and acclaim as usual.

Inside a week or ten days, you can start to include a touch of separation amongst you and your canine when you abandon him. When you do, utilize your left hand open with the palm confronting the canine as a stay flag, much the same as the hand flag a cop uses to stop activity at a convergence. Hold the sustenance regard in your correct hand as some time recently, yet this time the nourishment is not touching the puppy's nose. He will watch the sustenance hand and rapidly discover that he will understand that regard when you come back to his side.

When you can stand 1 yard far from your puppy for 30 seconds, you would then be able to start building time and separation in both remains. In the long run, the puppy can be relied upon to stay in the stay position for delayed timeframes until the point when you come back to him or call him to you. Continuously commend luxuriously when he remains.

Leave it

Numerous German Shepherds proprietors confront a great deal of inconvenience influencing their pooch to figure out how to leave a protest that they are gnawing onto. In the event that your German Shepherds is indicating terrible conduct by gnawing on furniture, pads influence them to figure out how to abandon it. Take after the tips beneath to transform your pooch into a dutiful one.

Grasp a treat and call your puppy's name.

When you get its consideration, drop the treat on the floor. Your canine will approach the treat and will endeavor to get it.

At the point when your pooch is going to get the treat from the floor, present your leg and put it in front of the treat.

Try not to venture on the treat, simply piece it.

Say 'abandon it.'

Again pick the treat in your grasp, backpedal a bit, drop the treat on the floor, call your canine's name, rehash the activity and request that your puppy abandon it.

In the event that it stops and doesn't take the treat in its mouth, pick the treat from the floor and offer it.

This will enable your pooch to relate the word 'abandon it' with remaining endlessly and will make it less demanding for it to learn.

Fetch

The intuition to pursue whatever you toss is all in your pooch's qualities. On the off chance that you're fortunate, your German Shepherd will play bring normally, in any case, just a couple of truly comprehend the idea of recovering. While canines will by and large pursue the toy, some won't bring it back.

Instructing your German Shepherd play get is an incredible approach to bond and mess around with him, and in the meantime a decent type of activity. Here are a few hints to kick you off:

Begin preparing him as right on time as could reasonably be expected. It is ideal on the off chance that you can prepare your German Shepherd while he's as yet a puppy. It is considerably simpler on the grounds that youthful canines are more receptive to new charges. Be that as it may, you can in any case educate more seasoned German Shepherd gave you have the tolerance to prepare him reliably, and obviously with the assistance of a lot of treats.

Pick a toy that is not sufficiently little for him to swallow and not sufficiently enormous that it can't fit into your puppy's mouth. It is suggested that prepare utilizing his most loved toys. Squeaky toys for the most part pulls in pooch's consideration.

At to start with, simply toss the toy close to the both of you, only a couple of feet away. At the point when your German Shepherd gets the toy, stand out enough to be noticed and call her to come to you. Bear in mind to commend her for lifting it up.

Rehash your instructional meetings a few times each day. Simply be persistent and your buddy will soon realize what to do. As you German Shepherd gets more acquainted with your get standard, you can attempt different articles like frisbee, a ball, whatever. What's more, obviously, dependably compensate her with a great treat and acclaim each time.

Stop the endless chewing

Have you ever had or currently have a German Shepherd puppy that adores chewing? Let alone on everything? A German Shepherd begins to gnaw at three years old to two months. This is the time when your German Shepherd puppy is creating teeth, a procedure known as getting teeth. Amid the getting teeth period, a German Shepherd pup will bite on practically anything that it finds. This conduct is a consequence of extraordinary gum torment that is dialed down when the puppy applies weight with its gums. Gnawing on things with over the top power will numb the gums, which won't cause disturbing torment.

Don not attempt to scold your puppy on his chewing, this will trigger more destructive behaviors. Simple attempt to correct it with plenty of chewing toys and keep your items away from his reach. Also try to correct this while your puppy is in his teething stage.

If the chewing gets to be too much or he is too stubborn, you can purchase anti-chew spray that will assist you in this critical stage of training.

Speak/ Quiet

Instructing your pooch to "talk," or bark on summon can be fun and helpful. Having your pooch bark on signal can be a fun trap to indicate loved ones. A woofing canine can avert interlopers and alarm you to potential peril. Exorbitant yapping can be a tremendous issue, yet educating the talk/calm charges can hone the normal nature to bark yet enable you to calm your pooch when required. With devotion and consistency, you can educate your puppy to bark on summon and to be calm.

Diverse pooch mentors and proprietors have changing systems, however here is one essential strategy that works for some mutts.

Trouble: Average

Time Required: 10-15 minutes, 1-2 times each day (may take a little while)

What You Need:

A pack of little yet delightful puppy treats

Your canine's most loved toy

A woofing boost (like a doorbell or a man to thump on the entryway)

Step by step instructions to Train Your Dog to Be Quiet

It's a smart thought to begin with the calm signal and ensure your puppy knows it before proceeding onward to the bark prompt. This is particularly useful if your pooch as of now likes to bark a great deal.

Make a circumstance that will make your puppy bark. The best strategy is to have a companion ring the doorbell or thump on the entryway. Or, on the other hand, you might have the capacity to get your pooch exceptionally energized with a specific end goal to cause yapping. Now and again observing another pooch can expedite woofing.

At the point when your canine barks, quickly recognize it by checking for the source (watch out the window or entryway, go to your puppy). At that point, stand out enough to be noticed (you may take a stab at holding up the treat or toy).

After the yelping stops, give your canine the toy or treat.

Rehash steps 1-3 yet bit by bit sit tight for somewhat longer times of hush each time before giving the treat.

Pick one straightforward word for the calm summon. This word ought to likewise be anything but difficult to recollect and utilized reliably. Great decisions: "enough," "calm," or "quiet."

Once your puppy has stayed calm a couple of times, include the signal. While your canine is yapping, say your tranquil order in a firm, discernible and perky voice while holding up the reward. Give your pooch the reward when the yelping stops.

Practice the "peaceful" signal often. You can do this whenever she barks, however continue instructional meetings brief.

The most effective method to Train Your Dog to Speak

Once your pooch appears to see "calm," it's an ideal opportunity to move onto the bark summon.

Pick one straightforward word for the bark charge. The word ought to be anything but difficult to recollect and utilized reliably. Great decisions incorporate "talk," "bark," and "talk." You can make up your own particular word or short expression, however ensure it doesn't sound excessively like another sign word or your puppy's name.

Indeed, get your pooch to bark normally.

As your canine barks, say your signal word in a reasonable, cheery voice.

Acclaim your puppy and give him a treat or toy.

Rehash the talk charge process a few times until the point that your pooch appears to get it.

Once your pooch learns "talk" and "calm" independently, you can utilize them together. Have your pooch talk a couple of times, at that point advise her to be tranquil.

Seek

Ask your dog to sit. Should your pooch not yet be able to understand sit, have a friend or family member hold him still.

While your dog is being held, go quite a distance away to the point that no one can see you, all while having a treat at the ready. Once you have gone, call you puppy and have your friend release the dog.

Once your dog finds you, congratulate and reward him with the treat. Because he is already dependant on you and is smart enough to realize it, he will soon get used to the exercise. Every time you do this, get further away and make yourself harder to find. This will teach your dog that every time you are found, there will be satisfaction as well as a chance for reward. This is a great way to get closer to your dog, but is also an essential skill for any dog that will be in the herding profession.

Discover It

Take your German shepherd's most adored toy. Play with him for quite a while and get him empowered, by then take the toy away and hide it. Have a friend hold your canine down as you do this. To start off, cover it in a certain place, for instance, in the midst of the floor in the accompanying room.

Return to the canine once you have covered the toy and say "find it" before releasing him. If basic, oversee him to the toy by walking around front of him. When he believes that its, spoil him with laud. Repeat this technique several times using straightforward hiding spots until the point when the moment that he gets used to the methodology.

Cover the toy under a couple of cushions or an old sheet, so he sees it before he sees it. It's basic for him to rely upon his nose, not his eyes, for finding the prize. Being herders, German shepherds are vivified by advancement, so you may need to ask him to get his nose to the ground. They are extremely smart, so ought to get new charges quickly.

Following

Take your pooch out into the yard or a secured stop. Drop a wiener on the ground and pound it into the ground with your shoe. This makes your shoe a significantly scented inquiry.

Leave your where your canine is playing. If key have a partner stay with him, or place him in the sit position. Walk around a dominatingly straight line, however hurl in a few sidesteps and twists to make the trail more inconspicuous.

Cover the toy in the grass. Return to your canine and give the "find it" charge. He will take after your tracks due to the have a fragrance like hotdog on the grass. Repeat this action until the point that he is used to the action, by then graduate to just contingent upon the trail of your shoes, rather than support, to pull in your pooch to take after the trail.

As he gets the hang of the beguilement, use elucidate trails, with curves, stops and circles, to make following all the more troublesome.

Leash Training

Depending on the age of your puppy, some will advise you to muzzle your German Shepherd incase he may get excited around other dogs, or nervous and lash out. Reframe from doing so as this is all new to your German Shepherd and muzzles can cause anxiety, and anger in your puppy.

Your German Shepherd will normally walk speedier than you. You aren't endeavoring to get your German Shepherd to stroll close by, but instead keep the rope slack before you.

The reason for a walk is to permit your German Shepherd (and you) to appreciate it – including sniffing, researching, getting exercise and outside air. Make sure to permit your pooch flexibility inside the requirements of your walk together – you simply need some level of control as the pack pioneer.

It is a German Shepherd's characteristic impulse (created in the wild before taming) to pull while being controlled, or battle against it. This might be the reason, when you battle your German Shepherd pulling with your own, it once in a while ever functions as an answer.

Preparing Tips:

Have some level of tolerance, and don't battle drive with compel.

You can play out this activity in your front yard, back yard or an open stop (or anyplace with some space) while your German Shepherd Dog or Puppy is on its chain:

Place your German Shepherd's most loved toy/question/bit of sustenance a short-medium separation in front of you both and start venturing or strolling towards the toy or protest (ventures for troublesome German Shepherds, and moderate strolling for further developed).

It's exceptionally straightforward – when your German Shepherd pulls, you stop and solidly however generously say 'No'. On the off chance that the pulling is reliable, you call your German Shepherd towards you and backpedal to the begin, removing your German Shepherd promote from its objective.

At the point when the chain is slack, you remunerate your German Shepherd with treats, or enable it to walk up to its most loved question/toy/sustenance.

The entire reason for this activity is to compensate your German Shepherd with encouraging feedback, and not proceed with commanding control.

Additional Tips

Pick your canine's name admirably and be aware of it. Obviously, you'll need to pick a name for your new puppy or canine that you cherish, yet for the motivations behind preparing it likewise considers a short name finishing with a solid consonant. This enables you to state his name with the goal that he can simply hear it obviously. A solid closure (i.e. Jasper, Jack, Ginger) livens up puppy ears— particularly when you put a solid accentuate toward the end.

On the off chance that he's a more seasoned canine, he's likely used to his name; in any case, transforming it isn't not feasible. On the off chance that he's from a safe house, they may disregard to disclose to you that he has a brief name allocated to him by staff. On the off chance that he's from a reproducer, he'll come to you with a long name, which you might need to abbreviate, or change. What's more, if he's leaving a harsh circumstance, another name may speak to a new beginning. However, we're fortunate: canines are greatly versatile. In addition, soon enough, in the event that you utilize it reliably, he will react to his new name.

New name or old, however much as could reasonably be expected, connect it with lovely, fun things, instead of negative. The objective is for him to think about his name a similar way he considers other awesome stuff in his life, similar to "walk," "treat," or "supper!"

Settle on the "house rules." Before he gets back home, choose what he should or shouldn't do. Is it accurate to say that he is permitted on the bed or the furniture? Are parts of the house beyond reach? Will he have his own seat at your eating table? On the off chance that the principles are settled on ahead of schedule, you can stay away from perplexity for both of you.

Set up his private nook. He needs "a room of his own." From the most punctual conceivable minute give your pup or puppy his own, private resting place that is not utilized by any other individual in the family, or another pet. He'll profit by brief periods took off alone in the solace and security of his sanctum. Reward him in the event that he stays casual and calm. His sanctum, which is frequently a carton, will likewise be a profitable apparatus for housetraining.

Enable him to unwind when he gets back home. At the point when your puppy returns home, give him a warm boiling water container and put a ticking clock close to his resting range. This emulates the warmth and pulse of his litter mates and will calm him in his new condition. This might be considerably more imperative for another pooch from an occupied, boisterous safe house who's had a harsh time right off the bat. Whatever you can do to enable him to get settled in his new home will be useful for both of you.

Show him to come when called. Come Jasper! Great kid! Showing him to come is the summon to be aced most importantly. Also, since he'll be coming to you, your alpha status will be fortified. Get on his level and instruct him to come utilizing his name. When he does, make a major ordeal utilizing encouraging feedback. At that point attempt it when he's occupied with something intriguing. You'll truly observe the advantages of consummating this charge ahead of schedule as he gets more seasoned.

Reward his great conduct. Reward your puppy or canine's great conduct with encouraging feedback. Utilize treats, toys, love, or piles of acclaim. Tell him when's he's taking care of business. In like manner, never remunerate awful conduct; it'll just befuddle him.

Deal with the hop up. Puppies love to hop up in welcome. Try not to upbraid him, simply overlook his conduct and hold up 'til he settles down before giving encouraging feedback. Never energize hopping conduct by tapping or lauding your puppy when he's in a "bouncing up" position. Walk out on him and give careful consideration.

Show him on "puppy time." Puppies and mutts live at the time. Two minutes after they've accomplished something, it's overlooked. At the point when he's accomplishing something terrible, attempt your picked preparing strategy immediately so he has an opportunity to make the relationship between the conduct and the remedy. Reliable reiteration will strengthen what's he's realized.

Debilitate him from gnawing or nipping. Rather than reproving him, an incredible approach to put off your loud canine is to imagine that you're in awesome torment when he's gnawing or nipping you. He'll be so astonished he's probably going to stop promptly. On the off chance that this doesn't work, have a go at exchanging a bite toy for your hand or trouser leg. The swap trap additionally works when he's into your most loved shoes. He'll incline toward a toy or bone at any rate. When in doubt, separate the gnawing conduct, and after that simply disregard him.

End instructional meetings on a positive note. Astounding kid! Great job, Jasper! He's strived to satisfy you all through the preparation. Abandon him with heaps of acclaim, a treat, some petting, or five minutes of play. This ensures he'll appear at his next class with his tail swaying—prepared to work!

Never Punish, Always Reward

Canines do recollect the past or they wouldn't wind up noticeably dreadful. Regardless of whether it's muscle or cell memory, pictures, scents, tastes and all the sensation recognitions of every occasion in their lives influence what they do in the hear and now. In some cases it just takes one injury, on nibble from another pooch, on whack with a slugger, to totally change a canine's perspective of his reality. Yet, recall that they do, as do we - possibly not every last bit of it in the conscious part of the psyche, yet it's altogether recorded some place. Those recollections influence our present and our expectations without bounds.

A receptive puppy, regardless of whether it is responding with flight or battle, is not dissecting the present. The pooch coming around the bend is NOT the canine that assaulted three years prior. The individual getting up out of the seat is not a similar man who swung the play club. The examination of current conditions is not there, just the response - the forecast without bounds and the shirking of the past. After for a little while, any piece of the past injury can trigger a response - a scent, a site, a development, a shading can entice a chomp. This must be made preparations for in light of the fact that torment implies passing is up and coming. A canine in this state is not living at the time by any means. This canine is anticipating the future in view of the past, stressed that something will happen. The responses from a pooch who is far gone down this street can appear to come absolutely all of a sudden. The canine has figured out how to regard everything as a risk.

More often than not, the creature does not comprehend that the conduct itself is what is causing the discipline, yet doing the conduct inside your arm's compass might be the factor.

The outcome is a pooch who proceeds with the undesirable conduct yet just when you're not around to see it. Then again, compensating needed conduct has demonstrated to make solid outcomes. This is on the grounds that the canine does the practices that prompts the outcomes, or prizes, that he needs.

Try not to surrender.

Preparing can be a debilitating errand, yet through safeguard measures, uplifting feedback and consistency you will have a solid and tried and true canine buddy in a matter of seconds!

Printed in Great Britain
by Amazon